T0022892

PUTTING BALLOONS ON A WALL IS NOT A BOOK

For Dad, and Ned—MJS

PENGUIN WORKSHOP
An imprint of Penguin Random House LLC, New York

First published in the United States of America by Penguin Workshop,
an imprint of Penguin Random House LLC, New York, 2024

Visit us online at penguinrandomhouse.com.

Library of Congress Cataloging-in-Publication Data is available.

Manufactured in China

ISBN 9780593662250   10 9 8 7 6 5 4 3 2 1 TOPL

Design by Lynn Portnoff

PUTTING BALLOONS ON A WALL IS NOT A BOOK

and non-advice

Inspirational Advice for Life

from
@blcksmth

TABLE OF CONTENTS

INTRODUCTION

Believe it or not, I haven't always been "The Balloon Guy" or even "Box Wine Boyfriend Guy." For decades, I didn't do anything creative and just focused on my retail management career. But there was a tickle in the back of my brain, an itch to create and make interesting things that just wouldn't go away.

About ten years ago, when I was approaching my fortieth birthday, I finally decided to give in to that itch and put my career on pause for a year to do whatever creative things I could get my hands on: I designed a couple of theater sets! I wrote and self-published a novel! And I started my account on a little photo-sharing app you may have heard of called Instagram.

My eye finally fell on Portland, Oregon, as an ideal destination to learn the ropes of being an artist. I used social media tropes as easy cannon fodder to make fun of for years, and then I decided to start using Mylar letter balloons (which are used in wedding announcement photos, birthday pics, anniversaries, you name it) to spell out quotes. See, I've always been a little obsessed with typographic art like the work of Barbara Kruger and Jenny Holzer, and I was already beginning to make fake flower petal installations to spell out truisms. When I started overlaying brightly colored Mylar balloons on contrasting colorful walls, I was so pleased with how the words popped off the screen: It was like shouting! The public seemed to instantly take to them, too: My friend Johnny Taylor Jr.

quipped that his whole life, he never saw balloon quotes on a wall, and one fateful day, they were *all* he saw online!

I eventually refined the way I made the flower petal installations (I use a drone to capture the photo now instead of a long clunky boom like I first used), and then folded the SpellBrite LED letters, which, while serviceable in storefronts, look ghostly and supernatural in natural settings, into my repertoire. I'm in the process of introducing another material to spell quotes with, so keep your eyes peeled for that.

It's important for me to tell you that I was *never trained in this*. The closest I took to art classes was studying the theater arts in college. And although my friends and family have all been supportive and proud, the advice from more distant acquaintances was "stick with one thing, and do that well" or "it's too late; you're too old to start an internet-based art career" or even "you didn't go to school for this? Better go back to school and study art."

This led to me listening closely, nodding sagely, and then promptly throwing out all that bad advice and just forging ahead on my own. It's my firm belief that everyone, yes, even you, Person Reading This Who Doubts Themselves, has an innate, powerful creative impulse inside them that only requires patience, collaboration, and curiosity to encourage into the light. And those naysayers? Well, I can't blame them. Perhaps they were discouraged from their creative impulses early on, too. We grow up to become the love—and the *fear*—we have known in life.

If you're new to my art, then welcome to the community! I get a few of the same questions from the curious every once in a while. People ask about the fine line any online artist walks between *art* and merely *content*. I say, why not both, and why has *content* become a dirty word? Isn't what you see in galleries and museums *content*, too? The question I get most often is, "Where do you source your quotes from?" The answer is some are original, but at the rate I make these installations, I mostly curate existing quotes that tend to slap me across the face. If it's something that stops you in your tracks, and makes you pause before turning the page, chances are it had the same effect on me! And yes, to address the sea turtle in the room, I do reuse these balloons from shoot to shoot. In fact, if you look closely, you can occasionally spot the first balloons I ever used, years ago, by the fact that I used to cut their poor little tails off.

I hope everyone who picks up this book, whether it's to give someone the gift of little nuggets of wisdom wrapped in Mylar or give themselves that same gift, knows how gratifying it is to feel like we're all part of this community who believes in the power of words. Words can transform, words can console, and words can provoke action and emotion. It's my sincere hope that these words bring you joy.

ON SELF-LOVE AND SELF-GROWTH

I am the worst. I write and curate amazing quotes, interpret them in a material I feel suits them, transform them with my art, and then release them into the wild. Some flourish, some stumble, and a few are weighty enough that I get DMs and emails thanking me for putting the advice or laughter into the world. All of this, and I am still the worst: because *I'm terrible at taking my own advice.* If I lived every moment of my life by the words I make art from, I wouldn't need to make art anymore! So why the heck don't I? Because growth takes time.

It's the most difficult thing, isn't it? We people with big hearts are so eager to find love under the most unlikely rocks, we dream of reconciliation with old enemies, we have fantasies of a world where love is unbound and freely given, yet we are the hardest on *ourselves.* We are stingy with compliments to the person in the mirror, and we hold ourselves to unrealistic standards. The "why" can be different with everyone; maybe someone grew up in a household devoid of compliments or affection. Maybe someone was told by a person whose opinion they valued that they weren't enough, and they believed them. Maybe someone was taught, however inadvertently, that a trait of modesty or humility was never to acknowledge one's innate beauty, grace, and greatness (I raise my hand, slowly at first, then more boldly as these *all* start sounding familiar).

No change that lasts happens overnight (okay, except oats). I wish it did, trust me, but a part of being human is doing it, getting it wrong, then doing it again until we get it right. When it comes to self-forgiveness and going easy on ourselves, well, *that* time is measured geologically. Celebrating the small wins of our own growth is so important, and so essential to building the momentum to truly loving the person looking back from the mirror, so why not start today?

SOMETIMES THE BEST GIFT IS THE PRESENT YOU DIDN'T KNOW YOU NEEDED.

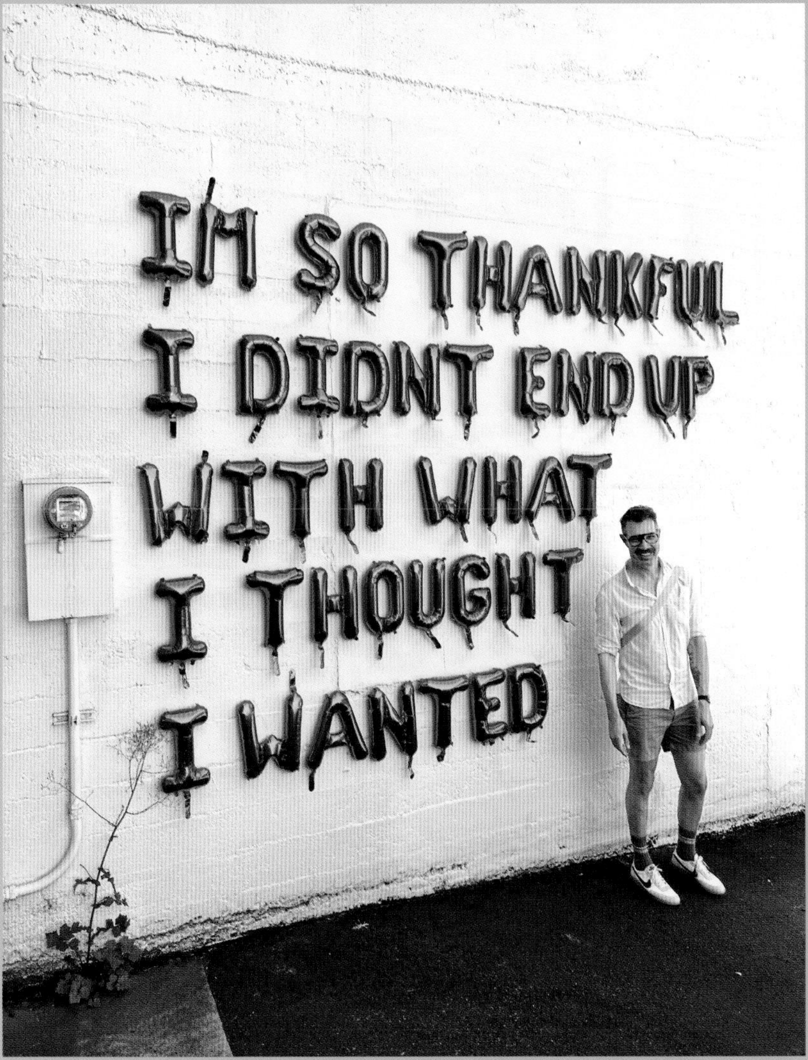
I'M SO THANKFUL
I DIDNT END UP
WITH WHAT
I THOUGHT
I WANTED

DON'T GROW AWAY MAD, JUST GROW AWAY.

—Quote by Maranda Pleasant

FOR THE RIGHT REASON, AT THE RIGHT TIME, WITH THE RIGHT MINDSET . . . JUST THE WRONG PERSON.

WHAT YOU DON'T KNOW CAN'T HEART YOU.

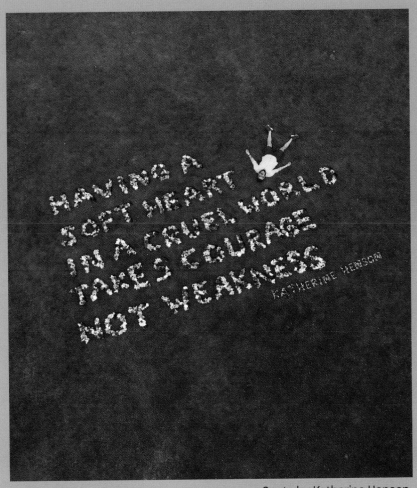

HAVING A
SOFT HEART
IN A CRUEL WORLD
TAKES COURAGE
NOT WEAKNESS

KATHERINE HENSON

—Quote by Katherine Henson

—Quote by Tony Goldmark

FOR WHEN YOU DOUBT YOURSELF

The reason that some quotes just shake us, or slap us awake, is because on some level, deep down, we already know the truth. Call it intuition, call it a hunch, heck, even call it a sixth sense, but we know that we have always been prepared for this moment and that no part of life comes with a road map. I think of my friend who gave birth recently, and she was perplexed when the hospital said "Okay, go home now!" with the new life in her arms but with *no instruction manual attached*. By and large, we learn the most when we make mistakes, and we need to remind ourselves that the only thing that's at stake is the act of making a mistake. We are human; *We learn by doing*.

Giving ourselves permission to feel everything: joy, sadness, fear, exhaustion? That's the key to quelling self-doubt. Feel it, deeply, and then remind yourself that everyone around you feels just as joyful, just as sorrowful, just as scared, just as tired. Those voices in your head saying you can't, or you shouldn't, are coming from the meekest part of you.

That's not to say there's no value in being cautious, frugal, or careful! The same human part of us that "learns by doing"? Well, it learned what not to do, too, by precedent. That's the frustrating thing about life and learning lessons: Time is annoyingly linear, and it's hard to ignore lessons of the past. In other words, fear is a completely understandable response to stimuli that produced a

YES, REST FOR THE WICKED.

—Quote by Anonymous, popularly attributed to Banksy

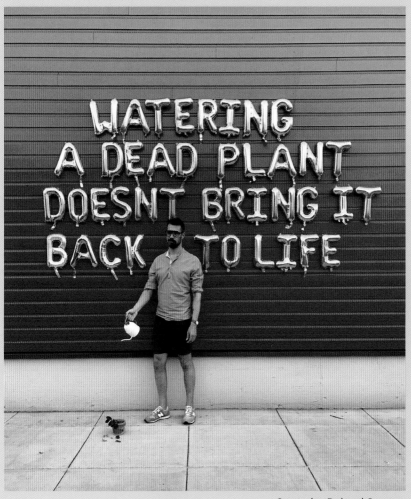

—Quote by Roland Sanner

THE THING ABOUT SURFACE TENSION IS THAT IT WORKS BOTH WAYS.

—Quote by Angel Alexis

Model: Sarah Jones

EASY DOES IT.

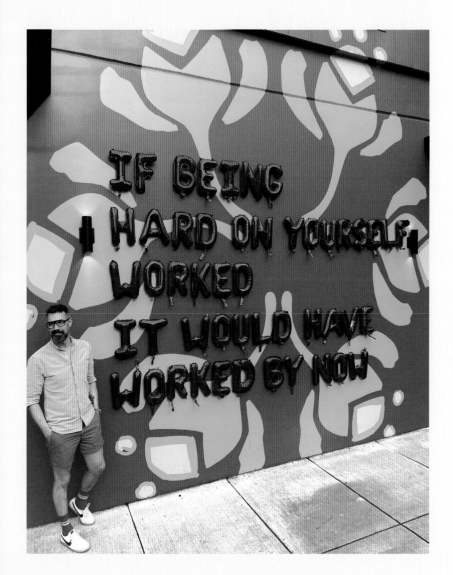

ADVICE FOR YOUR FUTURE SELF

Sometimes the reason words come across as powerfully as they do may not be because they fit us now. Sometimes we just aren't ready for the message. Sometimes we realize that the message may be for someone who doesn't exist quite yet. While some of the quotes I make art from are original and self-generated, my natural tendency of self-deprecation makes me lean on quotes curated from far wiser people than myself. I cast a wide net and find quotes that fit current situations and that strike me as presently profound. But I also skim for quotes about things I haven't yet experienced in my heart.

I review these files I keep, and sometimes a quote I curated months—even years—before can resurface like a message coming up from the inky liquid in a Magic 8 Ball. It's then that the words are the most profound: Nothing changed about the quote; it's *me* and *my circumstances* that formed to understand the quote. That's when I get the most excited because that's proof that I can change—that my neurons and brain matter have taken a new lesson from familiar words. This is a similar feeling to the one I often give other people with my art: Imagine someone who walks the same path every day, hikes the same trail, or goes to the same park. Suddenly, they turn a corner, and there is a message mysteriously suspended in midair, words blazing orange red in their sage truth. Or imagine that person walking down a sidewalk, and on a colorful wall nearby, there are overpowering words that fit their specific situation spelled out in bright, silly balloon letters. It's that same sense of discovery that *I* feel when a past quote fits a present situation.

Tasha Nassar said, "There is a past version of you that is so proud of how far you have come." It's an understandable instinct to look back on old hairstyles we sported, old fashions we wore, even old art we made and cringe. I used to, too, but I don't anymore. I love that dork! I feel deep affection for that person who was so eager and less world-weary than I am. I see what I was trying with my old writing and my dated art, and I love that guy for trying his best, and I love him for what he risked showing the world. What will future *you* love the most about your present self?

Will you remember that you were hard on yourself? And if so, how is that going for you? Will you remember your kindness, your empathy? Will you remember how eager you were to try new things? Will you recall the time you took a chance and it paid off? Will you recollect when you risked and you failed, but it was okay because you instantly forgave yourself? Will you remember the time you said no and that was the best decision for future you? Will you think back to the time you said yes, and it opened doors you never thought possible? Will you look back on the time you made for a parent, a sibling, a friend, or a lover even when you had something else demanding your time? Or will you remember the time you didn't do that and learned instead?

Words are powerful, words are gentle, words can sway thought and nation leaders and people with hearts both big and small. I hope these words on the pages ahead are my message in a bottle to your future self.

THEY'RE CALLED "ENERGY VAMPIRES" FOR A REASON. SOMEONE BRING ME THE GARLIC.

—Based on lyrics by Charles Aznavour and Marcel Stellman, sung by Nina Simone

Model: Sarah-Marie White

EXIT STAGE RIGHT

—Photo by Liz Eswein

TODAY IS THE BEST DAY TO START SOMETHING NEW.

FEELING DOWN? HAVE A GRATITUDE ADJUSTMENT.

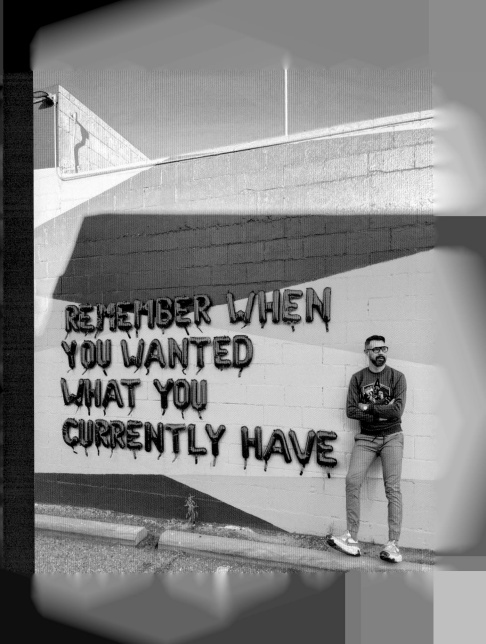

ACKNOWLEDGMENTS

There are too many people in my life to thank, but very sincere and special thanks to my family (looking at you, Mom and Linda) for always encouraging me to make more art, and pushing me to make the leap to be a full-time artist. Thanks as well to my tireless friends and helpers on shoots: Nolan, Izzy, Trevor, Jared, Corey, Cole, Nick, Niscelle, Travis, Michal, Peter, Chynna, Andrew, Tomy, Shawn, Esther, and Weston, who all definitely never shudder at the words "Hey, wanna help with a shoot?" Many thanks to Brian and Lauren. Thanks to my tireless video editors, Thomas, Krista, Ryan, and Tiera. Thanks to Jen for fixing my colors and my crunchy balloons. Deepest gratitude to anyone who has supported, shared, or promoted my art.